# How to p

# SNOOKER

## a step·by·step guide

**Author:**
**Liz French**

**Technical consultant:**
**Albert Stewart,**
**Secretary, Norfolk**
**Billiards & Snooker**
**Association and**
**Referees Association**

**JARROLD**

Other titles in this series are:

How to play SNOOKER
ISBN 0-7117-0504-6
First published in Great Britain, 1990
Text copyright © Liz French, 1990
This edition copyright © 1990 Jarrold Publishing
Illustrations by Malcolm Ryan

Designed and produced by
Parke Sutton Limited, Norwich
for Jarrold Publishing, Norwich

# Contents

# Introduction

Over the past couple of decades, interest in snooker has increased at a phenomenal rate to make it one of today's most popular indoor sports. Its success is largely due to the vast television coverage given to professional snooker, which has inspired so many amateur players of all ages and abilities. With snooker tables now found in many social clubs and even homes, the game is accessible to everyone and need involve no initial financial outlay.

Snooker is a game which can be enjoyed by all ages and at any level. At one end of the scale, a friendly game at the club offers an agreeably sociable pastime; at the other, a match between top players can demonstrate levels of skill, elegance and subtlety to make you gasp in admiration. Between the two extremes there are plenty of opportunities for

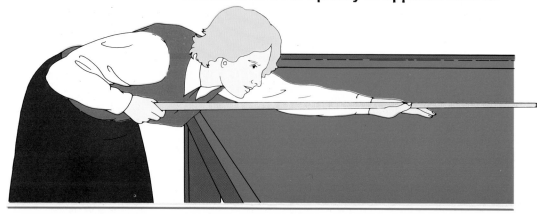

enthusiastic players to develop their skills and increase their enjoyment of the game.

Snooker clubs have opened up all over the country and joining one of these is a good step for enthusiastic players. As well as the social aspects, membership of a club gives you opportunities to play others and pick up tips and the chance to take part in local competitions.

This book takes you step by step through all the basics of the game, from how to choose a cue and how the scoring works to developing your accuracy and practising to improve your technique. If you are new to the game, some of the terms used may be confusing at first. When such terms appear in the text for the first time, they are printed in *italics* and are explained in the glossary at the back of the book.

Whether you aspire to become a top player or just want to beat your friends, you will find the game offers fresh challenges every time you play. Above all, snooker is a game to enjoy – so happy snookering!

# EQUIPMENT

## The Table

The standard full-size snooker table – or billiard table, to give it its correct name – is made to either metric or imperial specifications. The imperial table has a playing area of 11ft 8½ins by 5ft 10ins. This is slightly smaller than the metric version illustrated below and, for simplicity, referred to throughout the book. Smaller tables are also widely available and are very popular for private use at home and in pubs and clubs.

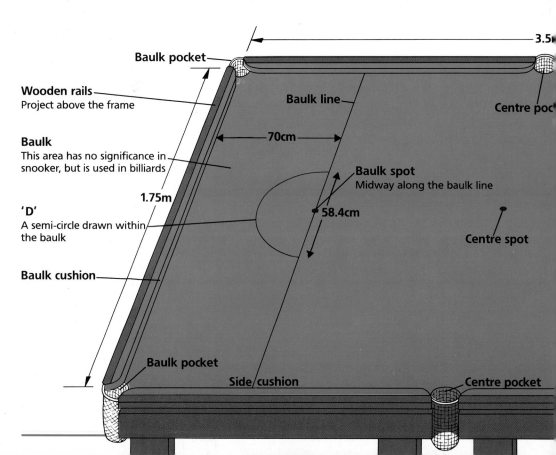

**Baulk pocket**

**Wooden rails**
Project above the frame

**Baulk**
This area has no significance in snooker, but is used in billiards

**'D'**
A semi-circle drawn within the baulk

1.75m

**Baulk cushion**

**Baulk line**

70cm

**Baulk spot**
Midway along the baulk line

58.4cm

**Baulk pocket**

Side cushion

3.5

Centre poc

Centre spot

Centre pocket

The top is slate covered with a tightly-stretched, woollen baize cloth with a thickish *nap*. There are baize-covered rubber *cushions* around the outside of the table and various markings, as shown here.

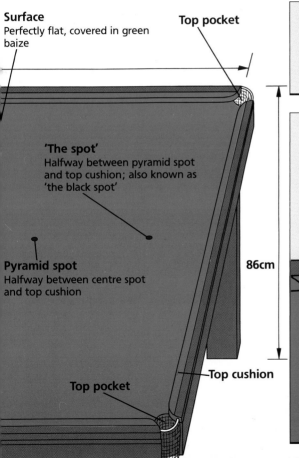

**Surface**
Perfectly flat, covered in green baize

**Top pocket**

**'The spot'**
Halfway between pyramid spot and top cushion; also known as 'the black spot'

**Pyramid spot**
Halfway between centre spot and top cushion

**Top pocket**

86cm

**Top cushion**

## Snooker or billiards?

Snooker is a relatively recent descendant of the Old English Billiards which uses three balls rather than the 22 used in snooker. Billiards is considered by some to be the more challenging game but snooker enjoys far wider popularity.

## Care of the table

If you are lucky enough to have your own table, a little regular care will greatly extend its life. The cloth should be brushed after every use to prevent chalk and dust building up in the nap and making the surface uneven. Brush the cushions first, and then from baulk to spot end, i.e. following the nap. Twice a week, iron the surface, again from baulk to spot, taking care not to damage the cushions.

# Cues

The *cue* consists of a thin piece of wood, usually ash or maple, about 1.5m long and weighing about 460 grams, though weights and lengths vary. The end held in the hand (*butt end*) is about 25mm in diameter; the cue tapers gradually to a round tip about 10mm thick onto which is fixed a leather *tip* for striking the ball.

A long cue of about 2.5m is supplied for playing shots along the length of a full-size table.

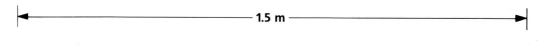

|← —————————————————————— 1.5 m ——————————————————————→|

## Choosing and looking after a cue

A wide variety of shapes, lengths and thicknesses are available and it is largely a matter of personal preference, of what feels and looks good to you. The most important point to check is that the cue is straight: look down its length or roll it on the table to make sure there are no slight bends in it. Check, too, that the tip is fitted flush. A *two-piece cue* is a popular and practical choice since its case is much smaller and easier to carry. A two-piece cue is also less likely to warp.

Remember:

● After using your cue, always wipe it with a damp cloth, polishing off with a dry one if you like.

● Always keep your cue in its case.

● Never leave it on or near a radiator.

● Never leave it propped up against a wall when not in its case.

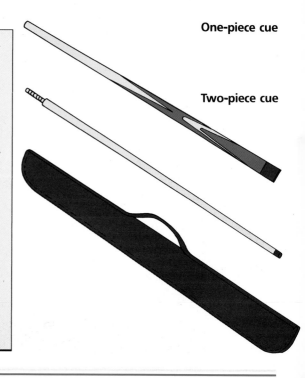

One-piece cue

Two-piece cue

# Other Equipment

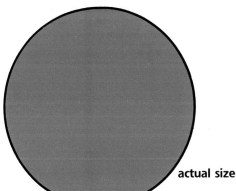

**actual size**

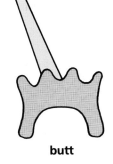

butt          cross          spider

## Rests

Sometimes access to the cue ball is restricted and for these shots a *rest* may be used. Rests are available in different lengths, a metal or plastic cross at the end providing a bridge for your cue. The *spider* gives you a bridge with extra height and is used when the cue ball is too close to another ball for easy contact. (See page 28 for how to use rests).

## Balls

Early snooker balls were made of ivory or even wood: these days they are made in a very hard and durable material called crystalate. 22 balls of equal weight and size (52.5mm diameter) are used in the game: one white *cue ball*, 15 reds and one each of the other colours — black, pink, blue, brown, green and yellow. The balls are placed on the table in special positions (see Setting Up, page 11). Each colour is worth a certain number of points (see page 10).

## Triangle

A plastic or wooden triangular rack is used to position the red balls at the start of a *frame*.

## Chalk

Chalk, usually green or blue, is used on the tip to improve its grip on the cue ball. Use chalk regularly but lightly.

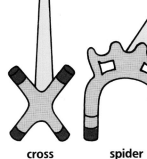

# SCORING & PLAY

# The Aim of the Game

Snooker is played by two players, pairs or teams — competitions are usually between individuals. Your aim is to score points by pocketing (or *potting*) all the *object balls* (balls other than the white cue ball) in the correct sequence (see page 13). At the same time, you aim to obstruct your opponent's attempts to do the same. Object balls may be pocketed only through contact with the white cue ball, which is struck with the cue.

# Scoring

A match is won either by scoring the most points or by winning the most frames. Points are scored when a ball is correctly pocketed. The coloured balls are each worth a different number of points as follows:

| | |
|---|---|
| Red | 1 |
| Yellow | 2 |
| Green | 3 |
| Brown | 4 |
| Blue | 5 |
| Pink | 6 |
| Black | 7 |

You also score points for *foul* strokes made by your opponent (see pages 18-21). Scores are recorded on a scoreboard, of which there are a number of types, both manual and electronic.

## What if . . . there is a tie?

If the score is tied at the end of a frame, the black ball is *respotted* (see page 13) and players draw lots for the right to determine who shall play the first shot at the respotted black. In matches based on points rather than frames, the tiebreak comes into effect only if the scores are equal after the last frame.

# Setting Up

At the start of a game the balls are placed on the table in the positions shown. The red ball at the apex of the triangle should be as near as possible, but not touching, the pink ball which is positioned on the pyramid spot. The cue ball may be played from anywhere within, or on the lines of, the 'D'.

## Playing order

You can decide who will play first by tossing a coin or using any other kind of draw. Once decided, the order of play stays the same throughout, with turns alternating between sides.

## 'On' balls

A ball is said to be *on* when you can legitimately pocket it. For example, after correctly pocketing a coloured ball in an opening break, you will be *on* a red.

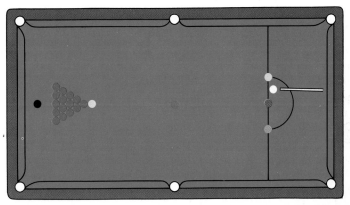

# A Stroke

A stroke starts when a player strikes the cue ball with the tip of his cue, and ends when all the balls have stopped moving. For a stroke to be fair:

**1** The cue ball is the only one you may strike.

**2** All balls must be at rest and, if appropriate, colours correctly respotted before the ball is struck.

**3** No ball must be forced off the table.

**4** You must not strike the cue ball more than once in the same stroke.

**5** At least one of your feet must be touching the ground at the moment you strike the cue ball.

**6** The cue ball must be struck, not pushed (a *push* is when the tip of the cue stays in contact with the cue ball after it has moved forward or after it has made contact with the object ball).

**NOTE:** If your stroke does not comply with all these requirements, it constitutes a foul stroke. The penalties for fouls are shown on pages 18-21.

# A Frame

You take it in turns to play, trying to complete as much of the frame as you can by pocketing balls in the right order. Your turn continues as long as you score with every stroke: once you fail to score, your turn ends and your opponent takes over the frame as it stands.

Consecutive scoring strokes in any turn are known as a *break*. The sequence for a full frame is given below.

**1**

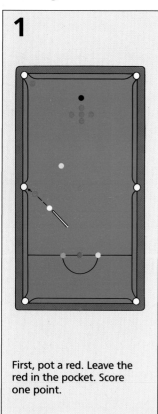

First, pot a red. Leave the red in the pocket. Score one point.

**2**

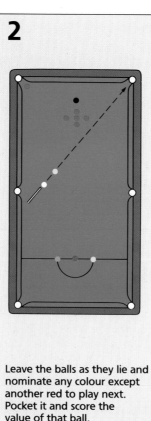

Leave the balls as they lie and nominate any colour except another red to play next. Pocket it and score the value of that ball.

**3**

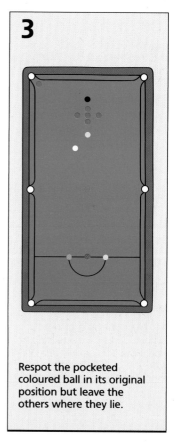

Respot the pocketed coloured ball in its original position but leave the others where they lie.

# 4

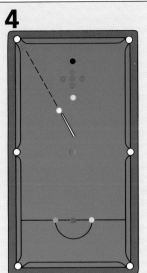

Continue like this, potting red and coloured balls alternately, scoring accordingly, respotting colours and leaving reds pocketed.

# 5

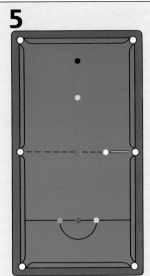

After pocketing the last red, nominate another colour, pocket it and respot it.

# 6

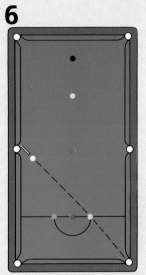

Coloured balls must now be pocketed in a set order: yellow, green, brown, blue, pink and black. The frame ends when the black is pocketed, or fouled, or when it is conceded.

## Respotting balls

Reds are never respotted. If you pocket a coloured ball, it is respotted in its original starting position except when clearing the colours at the end of a frame (see no. 6 above).

## What if . . . you can't respot a colour because its original spot is occupied?

Place the ball on the first available spot in descending order of value, starting with the black. For example, suppose you need to respot the yellow but its original starting spot on the right hand corner of the 'D' is occupied by another ball. Place it instead on the black spot; if that is occupied, on the pink and so on. If you can't respot the ball and all other spots are occupied, place the ball as near as possible to its own spot, in a direct line towards the top cushion.

# The Opening Shot

The first player places the cue ball by hand anywhere within the 'D' or on its lines. You are unlikely to pot a ball on the opening shot except by accident, so your main aim is to leave the cue ball in as tricky a position as possible for your opponent.

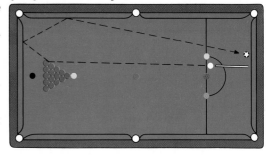

This diagram shows a common opener (or *break-off*) for less experienced players. Aim to make contact with the end of the five-row of reds: be careful not to hit the group too far in or you might hit the brown on the way back. The cue ball should end up on or near the bottom cushion or may rebound and end up behind one of the three colours in the 'D'. You could, of course, try the shot on the left of the reds. (For a more advanced break-off using *sidespin*, see page 39).

# Example of a Break

This will give you an idea of how a break a few shots into the game might go, and how it is scored.

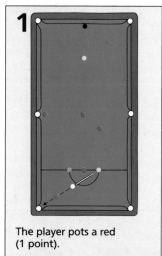

The player pots a red (1 point).

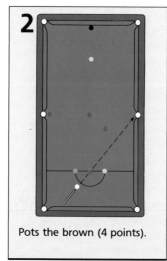

Pots the brown (4 points).

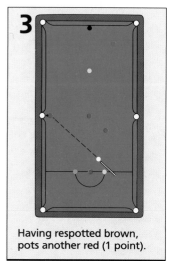

Having respotted brown, pots another red (1 point).

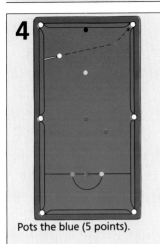

**4** Pots the blue (5 points).

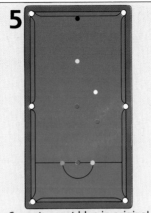

**5** Cannot respot blue in original position as occupied by red. So respots on black spot.

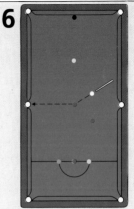

**6** Pots another red (1 point).

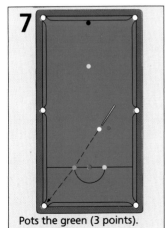

**7** Pots the green (3 points).

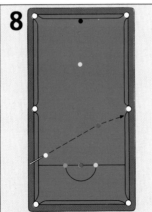

**8** Respots the green, but fails to pot another red. End of turn. Total break: 15.

## What is the highest possible break?

147. This would be achieved if you potted the black after each of the reds (15×7 + 15×1 = 120) and then took the colours in correct sequence (2 + 3 + 4 + 5 + 6 + 7 = 27). It has been done!

# A Snooker

This is, of course, what gives snooker its name, and it is an integral part of the game.

## What is a snooker?

A player is *snookered* if he cannot get at any on ball with the cue ball because the path has been obstructed by a ball, or balls, not on. This is a tactical stroke, mainly used in defence. If you are unable to go further with a break, a carefully laid snooker can prevent your opponent taking the advantage, and give you a good opening in your next turn.

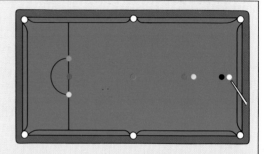

## What can you do?

When snookered, you **must** attempt the shot, usually by hitting off one or more of the cushions. You may be able to strike the on ball very lightly (*kiss* it) – just enough to count as a strike and avoid penalty points – leaving the cue ball in a tricky position for your opponent. It is even possible (but rare!) to get out of a snooker and pot the on ball. However, you are quite likely to either hit a ball that is not on, (diagram A) or miss altogether (diagram B).

Either way, you suffer the penalty (see pages 18-21), lose your turn and probably leave a good opening for your opponent (see also *Safety Shots*, pages 42-43.)

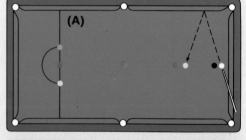

(A)

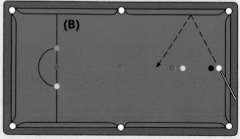

(B)

# Free Ball

**If a foul stroke from your opponent (see pages 18-21) leaves you snookered (ie unable to hit the on ball in a direct stroke on its extreme edges), you can claim a *free ball* as follows:**

**1** If you are due to play a red and all of them are snookered by a foul, you may nominate any other ball — this is called a free ball. This then counts as a red except that it is respotted if you pocket it.

**Example:**

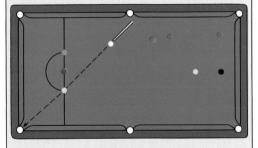

Here the two remaining reds were both snookered so you have nominated the yellow, pocketing it successfully. Now respot it and continue the break with any colour.
Score one point.

**2** If, once the reds have been disposed of, a coloured ball that is on is snookered by a foul from your opponent, again you can claim a free ball to count as ball on. If you legally pocket it, score the value of the on ball, respot it and continue with the break. This time you will still be on the ball you would have been on if not for the snooker.

**Example:**

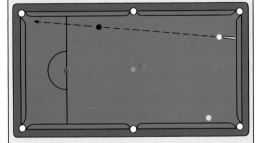

Here you were on green but it was snookered by a foul. Having nominated the black you pocket it. Respot black, score three for green and continue the break — you are still on green, of course.

---

**What if . . . after a foul, you pocket the nominated free ball and the ball on with one stroke?**

If the ball on is red, score two points, respot the nominated coloured ball and continue the break. If the ball on is any other colour, respot as appropriate, score just the ball on and continue the break.

# Fouls and Penalties

It is important to know what you may and may not do in a stroke so here the various fouls and their penalties are given. If you incur penalty points, their value is added to your opponent's score (and referred to as 'four away', 'five away' etc.). Your opponent also has

## 1 Potting the cue ball (going *in-off*)

**Penalty:** value of the on ball, or of any ball struck, whichever is higher.
**Example:** you are on yellow, and hit it but then the cue ball goes in-off. Four away because the impact with yellow counts and yellow incurs minimum penalty of four.

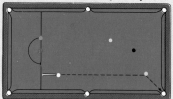

## 2 Striking or potting a ball out of the correct order

**Penalty:** value of the ball on or ball potted, whichever is higher.
**Example:** you are on green but strike black. Seven away.
**NOTE: For potting two reds with successive strokes, the penalty is seven points.**

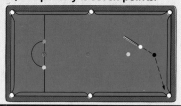

## 3 Playing a stroke with any ball other than the cue ball

**Penalty:** seven away.

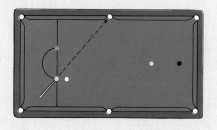

## 4 Playing before the balls have come to rest

**Penalty:** value of ball on, ball struck or ball potted, whichever is higher.

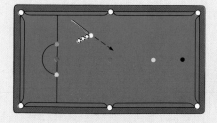

the choice of whether to play the balls where they lie or of asking you to take the next turn. NOTE: the minimum penalty is four points: the scores given here only apply if they exceed that. If more than one ball is struck, first impact counts.

---

**5** **Playing a stroke with both feet off the floor**

**Penalty:** value of ball on, ball struck or ball potted, whichever is higher.

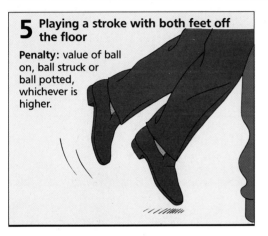

---

**6** **Forcing a ball (or balls) off the table**

**Penalty:** value of ball on or ball forced off, whichever is higher.
**Example:** you are on green and hit it but cannon into blue and force it off the table. Five away.

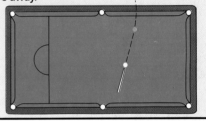

---

**7** **Pushing the cue ball instead of striking it**

**Penalty:** value of ball on, ball struck or ball potted, whichever is higher.

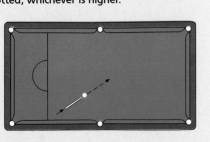

---

**8** **Touching the ball with anything other than the cue tip**

**Penalty:** value of ball on or ball struck or ball touched, whichever is higher.
**Example:** you are on a red and the edge of your sleeve catches the black as you prepare to strike. Seven away.

**9** Touching the ball with the cue tip before delivering the stroke

**Penalty:** value of ball on.
**Example:** while lining up to strike a red, the cue tip just nudges the cue ball. Four away.

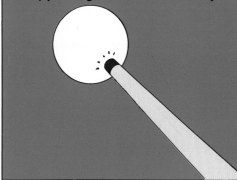

**10** Using a *jump shot*, making the cue ball leap over another ball by hitting it very low down.

**Penalty:** value of ball on, ball struck or ball potted, whichever is highest.

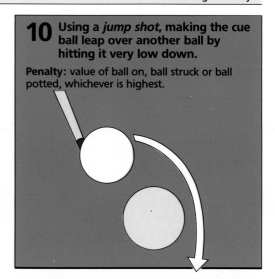

**11** Using a *dead ball* to test whether a ball will pass another, or go on a spot, or for any other purpose

**Penalty:** seven away.
**Example:** unable to see whether there is room for your cue ball to pass between two other balls, you pick up a red from a pocket to measure the distance. The referee may do this, but as player it is not allowed. Seven away.

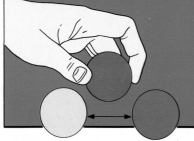

**12** Moving a ball which is touching the cue ball instead of playing away from it (see page 23)

**Penalty:** value of ball on or ball moved, whichever is higher.

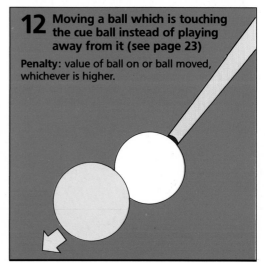

## 13 Not trying to hit any ball on (a *miss*)

**Penalty:** value of ball on or ball wrongly hit, or pocketed, whichever is higher.

## 14 Failing to hit the nominated (free) ball after a foul by your opponent

**Penalty:** value of ball on.
**Example:** you are on a red, nominate pink but fail to hit it. Only four away because pink acquired the value of the red for which it was nominated.

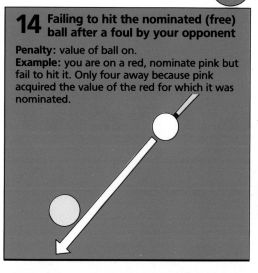

## 15 Snookering with the nominated ball after a foul, unless only pink and black are left on the table

**Penalty:** value of ball on.
**Example:** yellow is on but you have nominated black and snookered your opponent with it. Four away.

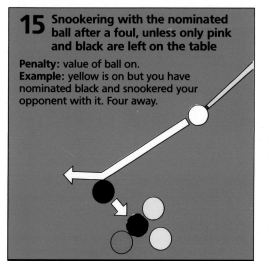

## 16 Striking two balls simultaneously unless both are red, or one is a free ball and the other is the ball on (see page 17)

**Penalty:** the higher value of the two balls involved.

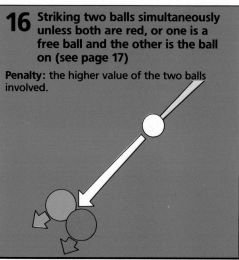

# Common Questions

There are a number of common situations which can arise and it is useful to know what the rules are. NOTE: This is not a comprehensive list: a copy of the Official Rules is recommended and available from clubs.

**1** If you force a ball off the table, it is a foul and is penalised (see no. 6, page 19). But what if the cue ball goes off the table?

This is also a foul, the penalty being the value of the ball on, or the value, if higher, of any other ball the cue ball may have hit. The next player plays the cue ball from anywhere within the 'D'.

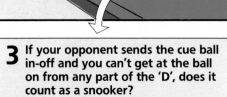

**2** If the cue ball goes in-off, it is a foul (see no.1, page 18). But what happens next?

The next player can play the cue ball from anywhere in the 'D'.

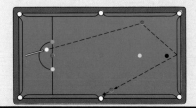

**3** If your opponent sends the cue ball in-off and you can't get at the ball on from any part of the 'D', does it count as a snooker?

Yes, and you can have a free ball.
**Example:** the one red left on the table is inaccessible from the 'D' after a foul. Take a free ball.

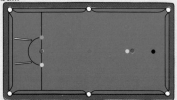

**4** What if you pot more than one red with the same stroke?

This is allowed. Score one point for each red potted.

## 5 What if you forget to respot a colour you have just potted correctly and continue with the next stroke?

This counts as a foul.
**Penalty:** value of ball on, or ball concerned, whichever is higher.
**Example:** blue has just been potted but has not been respotted. Five away.

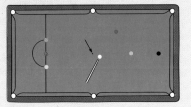

## 6 What happens if the cue ball is touching another ball?

The 'touching ball' rule can seem confusing. The first thing to remember is that you **must** play the cue ball away from the other ball without disturbing it, whether or not it happens to be the ball you are on. (see page 20, no.12). If you're **not** on that ball, you must obviously also strike the ball you **are** on, or it is a foul stroke. If you **are** on the touching ball, you must still play away from it but do not need to touch any other ball and can send the cue ball anywhere you like without penalty.

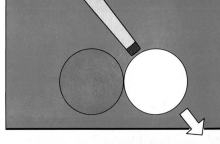

## 7 What happens if, whilst trying to pot a red, you hit it, then cannon onto another colour, knocking it into a pocket?

This counts as a foul (see no.2, page 18) and the penalty will be four points or the value of the colour potted, whichever is higher.

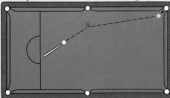

## 8 Supposing a ball is wrongly respotted, what happens if you play a stroke before you realise?

It is the player's responsibility to ensure that colours are correctly respotted, so this counts as a foul. The penalty is the value of the on ball, or the ball struck, or the wrongly spotted ball, whichever is higher.

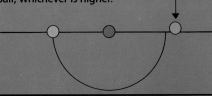

# POTTING THE BALL: PREPARATION

To be any good at snooker, you obviously have to be able to pot the balls — and that means developing a good cue action. Time spent on this is well spent because only when you can pot almost without thinking will you be ready to work on placing the cue ball for the next stroke (see pages 34-43).

## Holding the Cue

The most important thing to remember about how to hold the cue is that it should feel comfortably firm but relaxed. Do not grip too hard or your arm will tense up making your cue action less smooth.

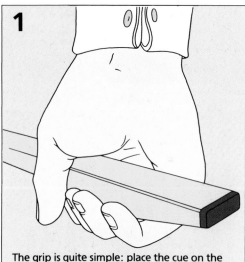

**1**

The grip is quite simple: place the cue on the table and pick it up about five centimetres or so from the butt end. The cue rests on the pads of the middle joints of all four fingers.

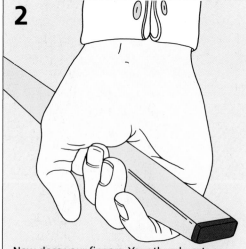

**2**

Now close your fingers. Your thumb rests on your forefinger. Only the thumb and first two fingers are actually holding the cue; the others help with balance and control. Your knuckles and the cue are in line with each other and the floor.

# Stance

**Getting your body position right is vital. Think about the position of the balls on the table and line yourself up for the shot before you get down into position. Remember:**
**1. The main aim is to get the cue in line with the shot. The whole stance is designed to keep the cue in that same straight line throughout the stroke.**
**2. Once you are ready for the shot, there should be absolutely no movement of any part of your body except the striking arm.**

Note: this diagram shows the ideal right-handed stance (reverse as appropriate if you are a left-hander). Your height and physical characteristics may make some minor adjustments necessary: if you are very tall, for example, you will need to bend forward more than a smaller person.

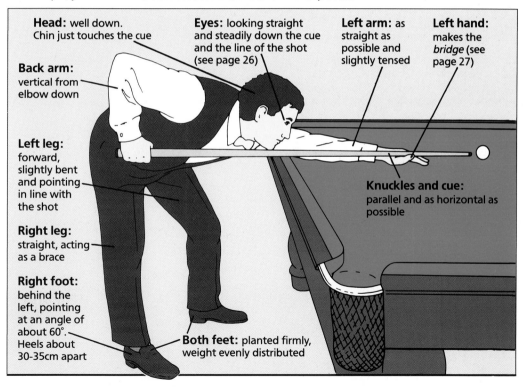

**Head:** well down. Chin just touches the cue

**Eyes:** looking straight and steadily down the cue and the line of the shot (see page 26)

**Left arm:** as straight as possible and slightly tensed

**Left hand:** makes the *bridge* (see page 27)

**Back arm:** vertical from elbow down

**Left leg:** forward, slightly bent and pointing in line with the shot

**Right leg:** straight, acting as a brace

**Right foot:** behind the left, pointing at an angle of about 60°. Heels about 30-35cm apart

**Knuckles and cue:** parallel and as horizontal as possible

**Both feet:** planted firmly, weight evenly distributed

# Sighting

The golden rule here is to get your head down so that your chin is immediately above the cue. Basically, you need to work out the exact spot to strike on the object ball, then keep your eyes fixed on that spot when you play the shot. Your head should stay absolutely still until the object ball is safely in the pocket or wherever you want to place it.

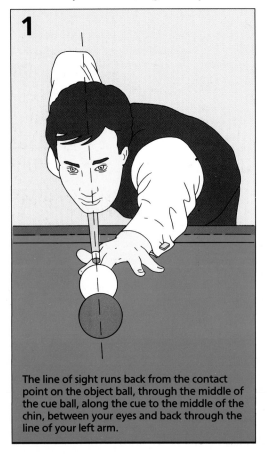

**1**

The line of sight runs back from the contact point on the object ball, through the middle of the cue ball, along the cue to the middle of the chin, between your eyes and back through the line of your left arm.

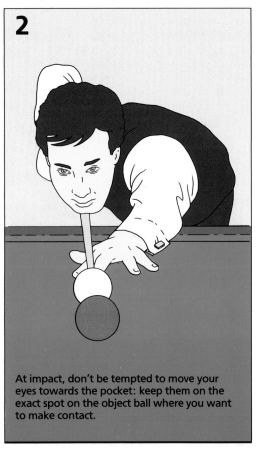

**2**

At impact, don't be tempted to move your eyes towards the pocket: keep them on the exact spot on the object ball where you want to make contact.

# The Bridge

**The bridge made for the cue by your left hand is a vital point of balance. Any movement of the bridge hand is likely to throw the shot off target so it must be firm and solid.**

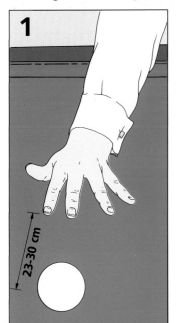

**1**

Once you have decided on your stroke and placed your feet, get down into position with your left arm stretched as straight as possible and slightly tensed. Spread your left fingers on the cloth. The bridge should ideally be about 23-30cm from the cue ball.

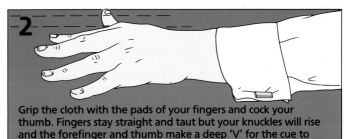

**2**

Grip the cloth with the pads of your fingers and cock your thumb. Fingers stay straight and taut but your knuckles will rise and the forefinger and thumb make a deep 'V' for the cue to move through. The height of the bridge is such that the cue will run parallel to hit the cue ball in the centre.

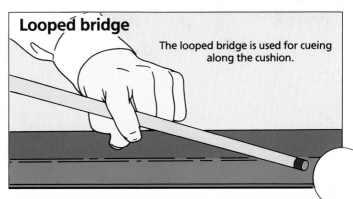

## Looped bridge

The looped bridge is used for cueing along the cushion.

### What if . . . your approach to the cue ball is partly blocked by another ball or a cushion?

In this case your bridge position may not be ideal. To get the best possible approach, you can vary the height of the bridge: lift your fingers to raise it or drop your thumb to make it lower (see also Using a Rest, page 28).

# Using a Rest

**If you cannot get close enough to the cue ball with your bridge hand, you can use the rest as an extension of the bridge. Since you will be unable to get down and sight in the normal way, you will have less control of the shot so take your time setting up.**

**1** Don't try to maintain your square stance when using a rest – move into the most natural feeling position. You will also need to adjust your grip. Most players find it easiest to have the thumb underneath and the first two fingers on top, using the third finger to add balance.

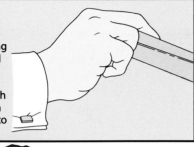

**Spider**

**2**

Hold the shaft of the rest down firmly with your left hand. The rest is placed at an angle to the line of the shot.

The spider rest is used if you need to cue over another ball. Note the upright stance and steep angle of the cue. You can really only hit the top part of the cue ball so the range of shots is limited and accuracy is not easy.

# POTTING THE BALL: ACTION

The movement of the cue is sometimes likened to that of a piston: straight, level and rhythmic. Your arm and cue should be the only things moving. Although the action appears as one fluid movement, you will need to consider its five elements: *backswing, pause*, hit, *follow-through* and stop.

## Backswing

This part of the stroke — pulling back the cue before it drives forward onto the white ball — is very important because it determines what happens to the rest of the stroke. The further back you pull the cue, the more power you give the stroke (see also Power Drives, page 41). But never use a longer backswing than you need: the further back you pull the cue, the further it has to travel, and the harder it is to keep it straight.

## Start of the backswing

Note the straight line made by ball, cue and right upper arm. Forearm vertical.

## Long backswing

The long backswing gives you more power but less control.

## Short backswing

The short backswing gives you less power but more control.

## Pace

Length of backswing affects the power of your stroke and, obviously, so does the speed with which you deliver the cue. How do you get it right? Unfortunately, there is no simple formula for judging pace: you will need plenty of practice before you can reliably predict how fast to deliver the cue for any particular shot. The general rule is — never use more power or pace than you need.

# Pause

At the end of the backswing, allow a momentary pause before driving the cue forward to strike the white ball. The pause gives you a final check on your control of the cue and is crucial for good timing and accuracy. When everything is balanced and perfectly still, you are ready to strike.

# Hit

Now for the actual impact of your cue with the white ball. Points to remember are:

● Only your right arm should be moving.

● Think of the piston movement and keep the cue horizontal. If the cue does not come through parallel you will be hitting either slightly down or slightly up on the ball.

● At the moment of impact your forearm should be vertical or near vertical. Your chin should be very close to the cue.

**What if . . . you are not making contact with the cue ball until after your forearm has passed through the vertical?**

You are probably standing too far away in relation to the cue ball. Move in a bit.

## Follow-through

Following through the shot with your cue is an integral and necessary part of the action. Again, concentrate on keeping the cue horizontal. How long or short the follow-through should be depends on a number of factors and varies from player to player. But if you get the driving action right, the follow-through should be almost automatic.

## Stop

When in the follow-through should you stop the cue? Again, this will vary according to the type of shot you are playing and it is something that will come naturally with practice and experience. Experiment and observe the different effects you can get on the white ball by stopping at different points of the follow-through.

### What if . . . the white ball always seems to veer off to one side before it reaches the object ball?

First, check all the basics of stance and technique covered so far. Remember that learning to keep the cue in a straight line is not easy: it is even harder to hit the ball dead centre too! The only answer is lots of practice — you will find some hints on pages 44-47.

# Straight Line Potting

**Now that you have considered the basic action of the cue, it's time to put it into practice and try potting a few balls!**

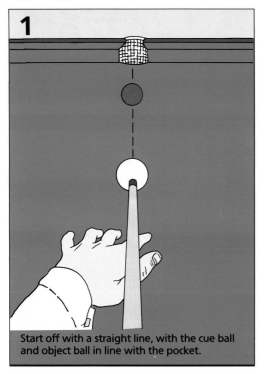

Start off with a straight line, with the cue ball and object ball in line with the pocket.

Concentrate on getting your stance right and the pot should take care of itself.

## What if . . . you keep missing the pocket?
Check through all the basics again:

- were you lined up properly?
- did you move some part of your body?
- was your sighting OK?

- did you keep your eyes on the exact point you wanted to hit on the object ball?
- did the cue stay horizontal and completely straight? Now try again!

# Potting at an Angle

So far the shots considered have all been in straight lines. But life isn't like that — so what happens when you need to deflect the object ball at an angle in order to pot it?

The basic point to remember is that, whatever the angle, the straight line is still there. You will always be hitting the white ball in a straight line. It is the contact with the object ball that varies.

There are three main angles (apart from the straight line, or full-ball) to remember: all others are minor variations on these. In each case, imagine a line drawn through the cue and the centre of the white ball to the contact point on the object ball. Note: these shots all involve hitting the ball dead centre.

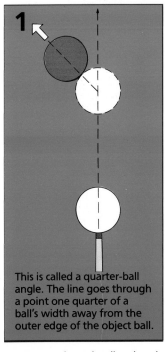

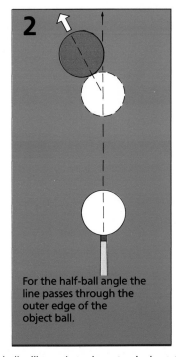

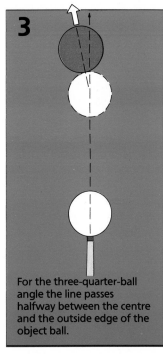

This is called a quarter-ball angle. The line goes through a point one quarter of a ball's width away from the outer edge of the object ball.

For the half-ball angle the line passes through the outer edge of the object ball.

For the three-quarter-ball angle the line passes halfway between the centre and the outside edge of the object ball.

The arrows show the direction the ball will travel at when struck along these lines, but try exercise no. 3 on page 45 to check for yourself what happens in each case.

# CONTROLLING THE CUE BALL

## Spin

Not until you are regularly and confidently potting balls can you begin to concentrate on positioning the cue ball for your next shot to build up breaks.

So far the shots learned have all involved striking the cue ball half-way down its imaginary centre line: these are known as *plain-ball* shots. You will have found with these shots that the white ball goes off at an angle after impact with the object ball: the following techniques allow you to decide where it goes.

Control of the cue ball relies on *spin*, the easiest types to master being *topspin* and *backspin*. Most other kinds of spin are variations on these two basic types and all need plenty of practice (see page 44 for practice tips).

### Topspin

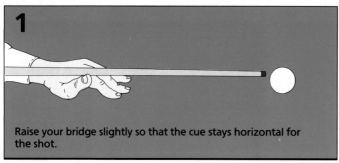

**1** Raise your bridge slightly so that the cue stays horizontal for the shot.

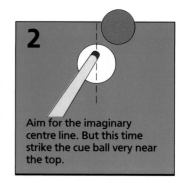

**2** Aim for the imaginary centre line. But this time strike the cue ball very near the top.

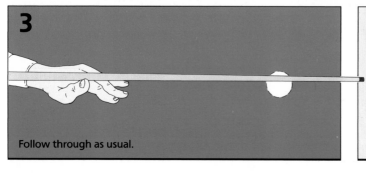

**3** Follow through as usual.

**Effect:** cue ball travels forward as usual, but gains extra forward propulsion from the topspin.

**Use:** when you want the cue ball to travel straight on from the point of impact.

# Backspin

Also known as screw, this is not easy to master, but with practice will be an invaluable addition to your skills.

**1**

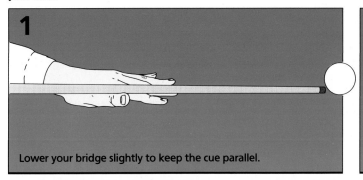

Lower your bridge slightly to keep the cue parallel.

**2**

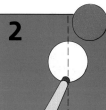

To impart backspin, again aim at the imaginary line down the centre. Strike the cue ball very near the bottom.

**3**

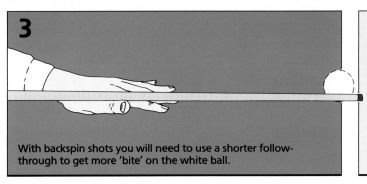

With backspin shots you will need to use a shorter follow-through to get more 'bite' on the white ball.

**Effect:** the ball travels forward but on contact with the object ball travels back along its path as a result of the backspin.

**Use:** when you want the cue ball to come to rest back towards you.

### What if . . . you're sure you are putting backspin on the ball but it doesn't come back?

Check that you are hitting with enough pace, and that your follow-through is not too long. Otherwise, chances are you are not confident enough about the stroke, and are hitting the cue ball higher than you should. Remember that if you hit the ball low enough it WILL come back. Once you have decided to use backspin, go for it — with a crisp, accurate strike.

### What if . . . the cue ball jumps?

This happens if your cue strikes the ball at an angle. Make sure your bridge is low enough to keep the cue horizontal.

# Stun

This is a variation on backspin. It is hard to master but worth practising. It is also closely related to the useful *stun run-through* shots described on page 37.

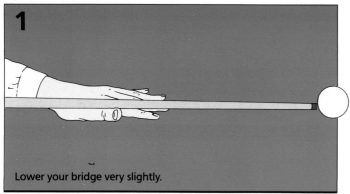

**1**

Lower your bridge very slightly.

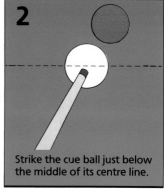

**2**

Strike the cue ball just below the middle of its centre line.

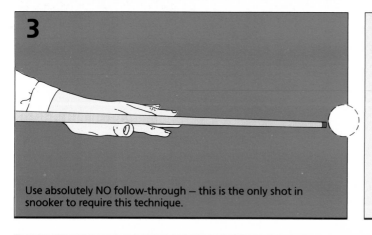

**3**

Use absolutely NO follow-through — this is the only shot in snooker to require this technique.

**Effect:** the cue ball will stop dead on impact with the object ball.

**Use:** when you want to pot or move an object ball leaving the cue ball in its place.

---

**What if . . . the cue ball runs on after impact?**

You are hitting the ball too high. Or you are inadvertently following through slightly.

# Stun run-through

Played correctly, this shot allows you to place the white ball in a wide variety of positions on the table. Somewhere between the topspin and stun, it is used by professionals and experienced players more often than any other shot so, although fairly advanced, it is well worth learning. You will need a good deal of practice before you can judge with any accuracy what will happen to the white ball.

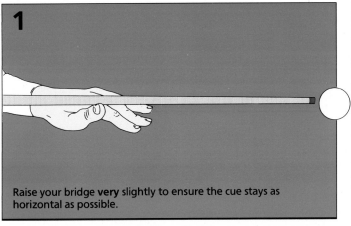

**1**

Raise your bridge **very** slightly to ensure the cue stays as horizontal as possible.

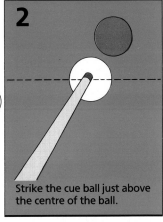

**2**

Strike the cue ball just above the centre of the ball.

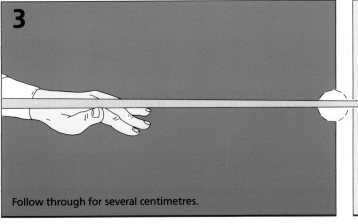

**3**

Follow through for several centimetres.

**Effect:** after impact with the object ball, the cue ball runs on with more control than either a plain-ball or topspin shot. Where it stops depends on where exactly on the cue ball you strike, the pace of your shot and the length of follow-through.

**Use:** to place the cue ball accurately around the table.

# Sidespin

So far all the shots have involved striking the white ball at some point on its imaginary centre line. With sidespin — or side, as it is usually known — you are aiming to hit the ball to one side. Sidespin can also be combined with backspin and topspin to increase the variety of shots possible. All these are very advanced techniques and accuracy is hard because you need to take the nap of the cloth into account. Travelling with the nap, the cue ball will veer in the opposite direction, but not so far off line. It is worth experimenting to see the different effects you get (see exercise 7, page 47), but do not expect to incorporate sidespin into your game for some time.

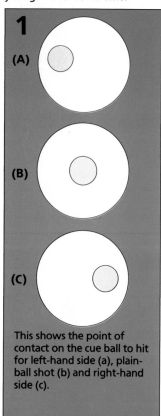

This shows the point of contact on the cue ball to hit for left-hand side (a), plain-ball shot (b) and right-hand side (c).

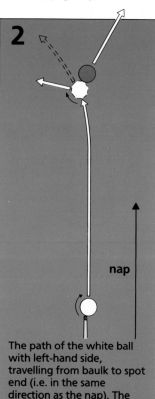

The path of the white ball with left-hand side, travelling from baulk to spot end (i.e. in the same direction as the nap). The dotted line shows where a plain-ball shot would travel.

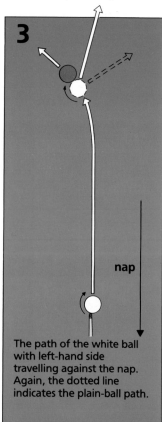

The path of the white ball with left-hand side travelling against the nap. Again, the dotted line indicates the plain-ball path.

**4**

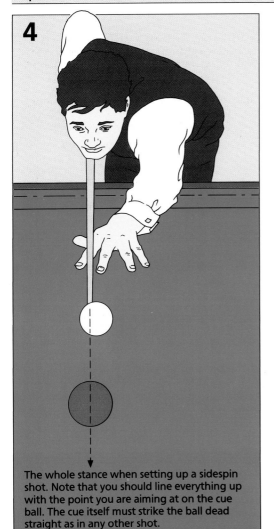

The whole stance when setting up a sidespin shot. Note that you should line everything up with the point you are aiming at on the cue ball. The cue itself must strike the ball dead straight as in any other shot.

# Break-off shot

The main advantage of learning basic sidespin technique early on is that you can use it for a more effective break-off shot at the start of a frame (see page 14 for the simplest break-off). Here, the target — the pyramid of reds — is large enough to allow for the inevitable margin of error present with sidespin shots.

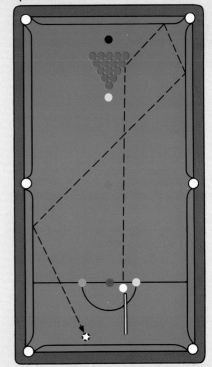

Break-off shot using right-hand side.

# Drag

**This is a variation on backspin which allows you to strike an object-ball softly from a distance. A plain-ball shot at a slow enough pace would almost certainly deviate with the nap of the cloth before reaching the object ball. The *drag* is an advanced shot which needs lots of practice.**

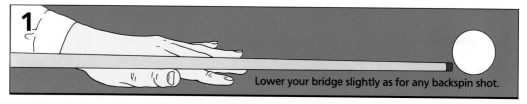

**1** Lower your bridge slightly as for any backspin shot.

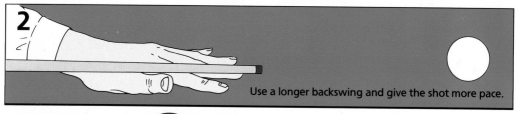

**2** Use a longer backswing and give the shot more pace.

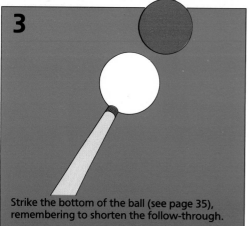

**3** Strike the bottom of the ball (see page 35), remembering to shorten the follow-through.

**Effect:** using backspin means you can hit the ball hard enough to avoid deviation on the way to the object ball which is some way up the table. The backspin wears off before impact and the cue ball skids over the cloth until it grips it, finally rolling gently forward to strike the object ball at the required pace.

**Use:** when your on ball is some way off and you want to hit it gently.

---

**What if . . . instead of rolling forwards when the backspin wears off, the cue ball just stops?**

You are not hitting hard enough. Lengthen your backswing and apply more pace (see page 29).

# Power Drives

A power shot or drive is one which uses maximum force. It looks most impressive but is never used just for effect — remember that the harder you hit, the less control you have. So the rule is always: never use more power than you need.

**1** Use a long backswing, bringing the tip of the cue right back to the 'V' of your bridge.

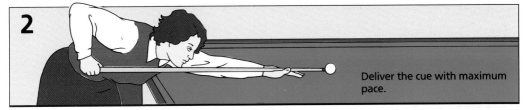

**2** Deliver the cue with maximum pace.

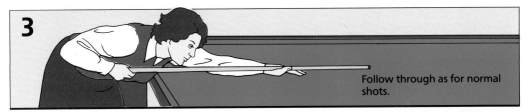

**3** Follow through as for normal shots.

**Effect:** is obvious! The cue ball moves very fast, strikes the object ball with some force, and rebounds off one or more cushions before coming to rest.

**Use:** if you need to place the cue ball in a position on the table which you can't reach with a slower pace. This is the ONLY valid reason for using the power drive. Even then don't risk it if the cue ball is more than about 45cm away from the object ball.

**WARNING: Power drives performed by inexperienced players can result in balls flying off tables or cue tips digging into cloths, and will not win you points in the popularity stakes with club owners!**

# Tactics and Safety Shots

**The most well-known defensive shot is, of course, the snooker (see page 16). But it is not the only form of safety shot.**

## Points to remember

**1** Your first aim has to be to pot the ball you are on. Once you have decided to try to pot a ball, go for it and be positive. But if you genuinely cannot continue with your own break, you can try sending the cue ball to an awkward position, or as far away as possible from your opponent's ball on, making his next stroke as difficult as possible. This is a safety shot.

**2** Remember that you must make contact with the ball on or you will forfeit penalty points. Of course, your opponent's response might be to bounce the ball back into an equally difficult position for you . . . but that is the nature and challenge of the game!

**3** Make it a part of your game always to look ahead and consider what will happen if you miss the pot you are going for. Will you be leaving the cue ball ideally placed for your opponent? Is there anything you can do to minimise the risk?

## Example 1

Here several reds were left on the table but no easy scoring stroke.

**Risk:** if you miss a pot your opponent is likely to have a good chance of a break.

**Solution:** rather than risk missing a pot, use a safety shot, sending the white ball far away from the reds to rest near the bottom cushion. Do make contact with your ball on, though, or it will be a foul.

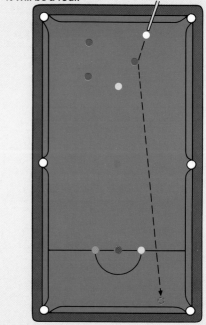

# Example 2

There is one red left on the table and it is a very difficult pot because the cue ball is some distance away.

**Risk:** if you miss potting the red, you might leave it on, thereby allowing your opponent to win the frame.

**Solution:** play a safety shot as illustrated, leaving the cue ball in baulk.

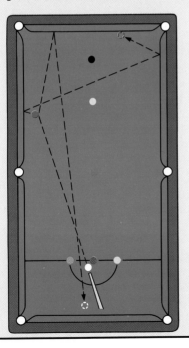

# Example 3

You have potted a red but finished just below the brown.

**Risk:** the baulk colours are all difficult pots and there is no easy way to get back up the table to the reds.

**Solution:** *trickle* up behind the brown. It is likely that even if your opponent safely negotiates the snooker, he will leave you in amongst the reds for your next shot.

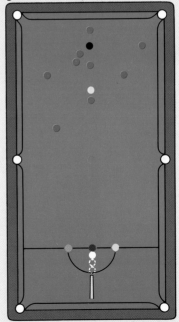

# Practising

These exercises are for you to try on your own and will help to improve your technique. Try to practise each one until you can do it without making a mistake.

## 1 Hitting in a straight line

Place the cue ball on the brown spot and practise hitting it up the table over the centre line spots. Concentrate on watching the cue tip rather than the ball: if your stance, sighting and technique are sound, the ball will pass over the spots, bounce off the bottom cushion and travel back along the same line.

## 2 Hitting an object ball

Now try a similar but much harder exercise, this time with the addition of an object ball placed about 30cm upline from the white ball. The aim is to strike the cue ball so that it hits the object ball and sends it up to the top cushion and back down the same line to kiss the white ball. As you get better at this, increase the distance between the two balls.

### What if . . . the ball travels up the table OK but deviates off line on the way back?

Your cue action is at fault here. Stance and technique are probably all right but if the cue is even the tiniest bit out of line you will inadvertently be striking the ball slightly off centre, making it deviate. Concentrate on your sighting.

# 3 Judging angles

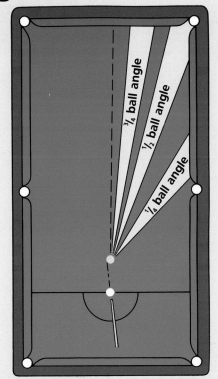

Place the white ball on the brown spot and another colour (say, pink) about 30cm in front on the same line, as for exercise 2. Now line up to hit the object ball on either side and at quarter and three-quarter ball angles (see page 33). What happens? Keep practising until you can reliably predict the path of the object ball — it should travel within the areas indicated here.

# 4 Potting at an angle (1)

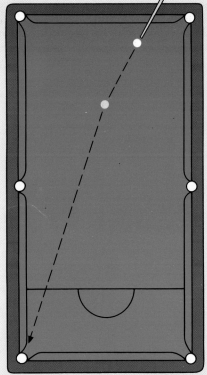

Place the pink ball on its spot and the cue ball near the top cushion just out of line with the pink and one of the baulk pockets. Work out the angle you think you need to pot the pink, then try it. If you go wrong, make a mental note of what happened. Was your basic technique or your judgement of the angle at fault? Return to this exercise until you can pot the pink from this angle three times in a row.

## 5 Potting at an angle (2)

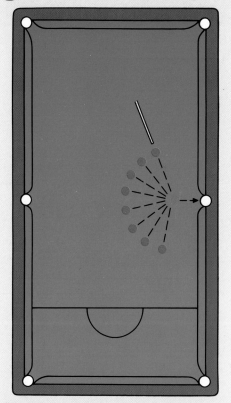

Place the blue about 30cm from a centre pocket. Arrange eight reds as cue balls in an arc about 60cm from the blue. Having potted the blue from all eight angles, move the blue onto its spot and start again. With the blue further from the pocket, you'll need greater accuracy.

## 6 Pot the blue

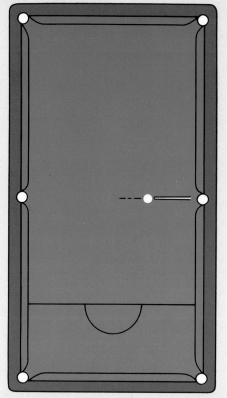

Start with the blue on its spot and the cue ball about 30cm away in a straight line with the centre pocket. See how many times you can pot the blue into either centre pocket. The blue, of course, is respotted each time, but you must play the cue ball from where it lies. It's harder than you think.

# 7 The line-up

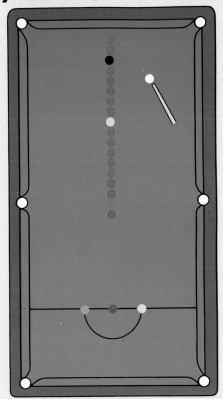

With the colours on their spots and the reds in a line down the table make as big a break as you can, potting reds and colours alternately and respotting the colours as normal. You may start with the cue ball in any position you like.

# 8 Spin practice

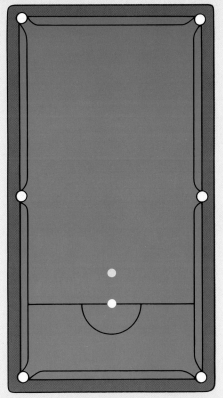

Set up the pink and white balls as for exercise 3. Now try applying the various spins – topspin, backspin, stun, stun run-through and side (see pages 34-39). What happens to the white ball after contact with the pink? Practise until you are sure the response is always predictable.

# Glossary

**BACKSPIN** Backward rotary motion put on a ball to influence its path.

**BACKSWING** Part of the stroke during which the *cue* is drawn back before the forward drive.

**BALL ON** See *on ball*.

**BAULK** The area of the table enclosed by the *baulk line*.

**BAULK LINE** Line drawn across the width of the table 70cm from the bottom *cushion*.

**BAULK SPOT** Spot in the middle of the *baulk line*; also known as the brown spot.

**BREAK** A series of consecutive scoring strokes.

**BREAK-OFF** The opening stroke which 'breaks up' the pyramid of red balls.

**BRIDGE** The support made by your left hand (right if you are left-handed) on the table for the *cue* to pass through.

**BUTT** The end of the *cue* which is held in your hand.

**CENTRE SPOT** Spot equidistant from the top and bottom *cushions*; also known as the blue spot.

**CUE** The long wooden tapered shaft used for striking the ball.

**CUE BALL** The white ball which has to be struck with every stroke and is used to strike the *object balls*.

**CUSHIONS** Baize-covered rubber running all round the inside of the table except at the pockets.

**'D'** Semi-circle drawn around the centre of the baulk, with 29.2cm radius.

**DEAD BALL** A ball which has been pocketed and has no further part to play in the *frame*.

**DRAG** A variation on *backspin* used when the *object ball* is positioned some distance from the *cue ball*.

**FOLLOW-THROUGH** The continuation phase of the stroke after impact with the *object ball*.

**FOUL** A stroke which does not conform to rules and incurs penalty points.

**FRAME** The complete sequence of play, from the opening *break-off* to potting the black. A match can consist of one or many more frames.

**FREE BALL** One nominated by a player to play instead of the *'on' ball* if the latter has been *snookered* by a *foul* stroke from the opponent.

**IN-OFF** The cue ball is said to go 'in-off' if it is pocketed illegally.

**JUMP SHOT** *Foul* stroke where the *cue ball* leaps over another ball.

**KISS** To touch the *object ball* very lightly with the *cue ball*.

**MISS** A *foul* stroke where the referee considers the striker has not endeavoured to hit the ball on.

**NAP** The raised surface of the cloth, running from *baulk* to *spot* end.

**OBJECT BALL** The ball you are aiming to hit with the *cue ball*.

**'ON' BALL** The ball you are due to hit, otherwise known as ball on.

**PAUSE** The phase of a stroke between the end of the *backswing* and the start of the drive forward.

**PLAIN-BALL** A stroke where the *cue ball* hits the *object ball* dead centre.

**PLANT** A position in which one *object ball* is played onto another with the aim of potting the latter.

**POT** To send a ball into a pocket.

**PUSH STROKE** A *foul* stroke where the *cue* remains in contact with the *cue ball* after striking it.

**PYRAMID SPOT** Spot half way between the *centre spot* and the top *cushion*; also known as the pink spot.

**RAILS** Raised wooden surrounds on the table.

**RESPOT** To replace a coloured ball on its original spot.

**REST** Device used to create a *bridge* for inaccessible shots.

**SAFETY SHOT** A defensive stroke used to send the *cue ball* to a disadvantageous position for your opponent.

**SIDESPIN** Sideways motion imparted on a ball by striking it on one side to affect its path.

**SNOOKER** To place the *cue ball* in such a place as to make the opponent's *'on' ball* inaccessible to him.

**SPIDER BRIDGE** A type of *rest* with extra height.

**SPIN** See *backspin, sidespin*, and *topspin*.

**SPOT** (noun) The top spot on the table, usually called the black spot. (verb) See *respot*.

**STUN** A form of *backspin* which causes the *cue ball* to stop after impact with the *object ball*.

**STUN RUN-THROUGH** A form of *spin* used to position the *cue ball* accurately.

**TIP** The end of the *cue*, covered in leather, used to strike the *cue ball*.

**TOPSPIN** Exaggerated forward rotary motion placed on a ball to influence its path.

**TRICKLE** To play the cue ball very gently into another.

**TWO-PIECE CUE** A *cue* made up of two shorter pieces which screw together.

Printed in Italy